How To Not Be Jealous

The Ultimate Guide on How to Overcome Envy & Jealosy

Mary Peterson

Table of Contents

Chapter 1

Recognizing Jealousy

Jealousy is a complicated emotion. While the emotion is complex, it is also extremely common. It's safe to say that we've all experienced jealousy at some point in our lives. When someone is jealous, they may experience a wide range of emotions, including anger, skepticism, embarrassment, and everything in between. If all of this talk about feelings and emotions hasn't made it clear, jealousy is entirely psychological.

Many factors can lead to jealousy. The most common trigger is when a person perceives a personal threat directed at a relationship that they value. There is a sense of being replaced with this threat, which originates from a third party. Our brains frequently associate jealousy with romantic relationships. For instance, consider a boyfriend who starts an argument because his girlfriend receives a text message from another man. Or maybe when we see an ex with their arm around someone new. These are common triggers for a jealous person, but we can also feel threatened in non-romantic relationships, such as friendships, coworkers, family members, and so on.

Some people are more susceptible to envy than others. *The following psychological factors may contribute to a jealous personality type:*

> - *Self-esteem issues*
> - *Anxiety, irritability, and depression*
> - *Possessiveness-insecurities*
> - *Fear of being abandoned*
> - *Codependency*
> - *Attachment style that is anxious*

Jealousy is likely not a foreign emotion for someone whose personality is clouded by any or all of these factors. This can make it difficult for them to maintain long-term meaningful romantic and friendly relationships.

As previously stated, there are psychological disorders and conditions that can make someone more prone to jealousy. There are various levels of instability within that. A low-esteem woman in her early twenties may occasionally feel jealous of others because she perceives herself as unworthy. A man in his late 40s may go insane when his girlfriend starts texting a new male friend because of the fear of abandonment he developed when his mother left him when he was a small child. We all have struggles, but how we acknowledge them determines how we show up for others.

While jealousy is not always the result of something "real," it can be! There are times when jealousy should be suppressed and personal feelings should be removed from situations. But there are times when our feelings of jealousy reveal something to us. Jealousy could be a warning sign of a failing relationship. Perhaps we didn't realize we were disappointing a partner, friend, sibling, or coworker until they found what we offered them elsewhere. According to some experts, jealousy is a necessary emotion to experience because it motivates us to be better and maintain our important relationships.

While jealousy can sometimes open someone's mind and ultimately be beneficial, it can also be harmful. Jealousy can destroy a relationship, whether they are the jealous party or the victim of it. This situation occurs when jealousy is unwarranted. Jealousy frequently causes problems that would not otherwise exist. For instance, if there is no reason to be concerned. Is the person who is jealous simply insecure?

Jealousy can also be detrimental to one's mental health. This frequently occurs when someone becomes far too obsessed with their jealousy issues. This includes stalking in person and/or online, judging others, being obsessive on their phone or computer, and other behaviors.

When a person is jealous, their thoughts may become obsessive. These behaviors can exist on a variety of levels and can be harmful to both parties involved. Obsessive jealousy can lead to someone obsessively watching another person's every move. From who they are speaking to, to where they are, to how they act and speak. There is a chance that someone in this mental state could turn violent. Did you know that one of the leading causes of domestic violence is jealousy? When there are many emotions at play, jealousy can become an even more difficult emotion to deal with.

Because jealousy can be caused by a variety of factors, there is no universal "cure" for the emotion. The most important part is simply acknowledging that the emotion exists and that it is clouding your mind. Jealousy is natural, but it can be difficult to manage. Understanding why we felt triggered and uncovering the emotions that led up to it can be extremely beneficial. When did I start feeling like this? What makes me feel threatened? Is there something that's missing? Which facets of me are responsible for this jealousy?

To better understand and address jealous feelings, we must first investigate what causes them. Jealousy is frequently rooted in insecurities and fears that a person is unaware of. Fear of oversimplification, fear of inadequacy, fear of being abandoned, fear of being replaced, and fear of being judged are examples of such fears. By recognizing what lies beneath jealous behaviors, we can better manage them.

It is critical that we change our perspective and recognize jealousy as a sign of emotional insecurity. This emotional insecurity can be caused by a variety of factors and can be detrimental to your mental health. Recognizing our insecurities and why we feel jealous is an important step toward managing our emotions in a healthier manner.

When experiencing jealous feelings, it is critical to express them in a non-confrontational manner. This can assist you in clarifying your feelings or concerns and addressing any potential issues before they become too overwhelming. This can also contribute to a healthier and stronger bond between people by allowing for understanding, trust, and respect.

While there is no magical cure for jealousy, it can be studied and avoided in the future. To get to this point, you may need to practice mindfulness, and therapy, challenge your negative thoughts, have intimate conversations, and be honest.

As mentioned earlier, everyone has experienced jealousy at some point in their lives. Although our psychological makeup makes us more likely to feel jealous, the emotion does not discriminate based on age, gender, ethnicity, or any other possible factor. Both men and women are motivated by a fear of losing something valuable to them. However, some experts believe that women are more likely to experience jealousy. According to experts, this is simply due to a woman's ability to be more in touch with her emotions. Compared to men, women are more receptive and sensitive.

While we may easily associate those two emotions, they are not synonymous. Both emotions elicit similar feelings in us, but they operate on different levels. When someone is jealous, a third party is threatening what they believe to be theirs. For example, your best friend met a new friend at work and is now going out to dinner without you. Envy is an emotion shared by only two people. When you are envious, all you want is what someone else has. This could be in terms of appearance, money, job status, class, and so on.

An animal must have some level of cognitive ability to recognize the importance of relationships in their lives in order to feel jealousy. While we have always struggled to fully comprehend the animal's mind, we do know that they are not too dissimilar to us. While it is impossible to fully identify emotions in animals, jealousy is thought to be a primal emotion. This implies that animals, at some level, experience jealousy. If you have dogs or cats, this is probably not shocking to you. When a new puppy arrives, we've all seen our dog become insanely jealous. But this is unquestionably a series of emotions in the wild! While these emotions are simple to define and recognize, they can be difficult to manage.

Identifying Jealousy and Envy

Jealousy is commonly associated with relationships, particularly with partners. Envy is more commonly associated with wishing for what someone else has or has accomplished.

Signs of Jealousy

Trust is an essential component of any relationship. A lack of trust can lead to negative thoughts when you are jealous. The following are symptoms of jealousy:

> ➤ *When you're not together, you don't trust your partner.*
> ➤ *When they mention other people, you become concerned.*
> ➤ *You're always checking their social media to see what they're up to.*
> ➤ *You suspect they're having an affair*
> ➤ *You're attempting to exert control over the behavior of your partner.*

If you are the object of jealousy, you may feel as if someone is attempting to take control of your life. They may check in on you, try to tell you what to do or not do, and how to act or limit your contact with colleagues and friends.

Signs of Envy

Healthy competition among people can be beneficial, but if you are unhappy when others achieve success or feel the need to constantly outdo them, you may be suffering from envy. Envy manifests in the following ways:

> ➤ *You're not happy for others when they succeed.*
> ➤ *The success of other individuals makes you unhappy.*
> ➤ *You feel compelled to diminish the success of others.*
> ➤ *You pass negative judgment on others.*
> ➤ *When others suffer setbacks, you rejoice.*

The rise of social media has been shown to cause envy and lower mental health in some people. When friends share photos of their best moments, it can evoke feelings of inadequacy or regret in others. These are strong feelings.

Chapter 2

The Effects of Unchecked Jealousy

Jealousy in relationships can be extremely damaging because it can trigger a variety of negative feelings and behaviors. Jealousy is motivated by a fear of losing something, and in the context of a relationship, this fear frequently manifests as a fear of losing a partner's love or devotion.

Jealousy is a destructive emotion that stems from negative thoughts and assumptions. One major reason why jealousy is harmful is that when a person is jealous, they may begin to doubt their partner's devotion or integrity, even if there is no evidence to support their suspicions.

Most notably, spouse jealousy can be extremely damaging to a relationship. When one partner is envious of the other, they may become dominant, possessive, and even aggressive toward their spouse. This can lead to feelings of being alone worry, and despair in the other spouse, eventually resulting in a schism.

Understand that there are different levels of jealousy and that some jealousy is normal in most relationships. When your partner openly flirts with someone else, for example, a healthy dose of jealousy kicks in. It's natural to find yourself confronting them.

When jealousy becomes excessive or uncontrollable, it can be a major source of conflict and sorrow.

Jealousy Can Ruin Relationships In A Variety Of Ways

Do you want to know how jealousy destroys relationships? These are the five proven ways it can harm any relationship.

Lack of faith

Jealousy causes partners to lose trust, communicate ineffectively, and lose emotional connection.

Controlling behavior, emotional distance, and insecurity are just a few ways jealousy destroys relationships, ultimately leading to a breakup or worse. While jealousy is natural, it must be dealt with in a healthy and constructive manner.

Managing Behavior

In relationships, jealousy can lead to feelings of insecurity, distrust, and domineering behavior. It can also result in emotional alienation and, ultimately, the end of a relationship. When this occurs, the aggrieved partner attempts to place the victim in a chokehold and begins closely monitoring them.

They would do everything possible to limit their interaction with others. If left unchecked, this quickly becomes toxic.

Insecurity

Jealousy in relationships can wreak havoc by destroying trust and instilling fear in the victim. When you try to control your partner, they may begin to withdraw from you. This can lead to insecurity and a loss of faith in your good intentions toward them.

Emotional separation

Jealousy can have a significant impact on relationships, causing interaction, confidence, and emotional connection to break down. When jealousy in a relationship goes unchecked, it can create a toxic climate of distrust and emotional distance. How do you trust and connect deeply with someone who is attempting to choke you?

You may eventually convince yourself that staying emotionally and physically away from them is the only way out.

Communication breaks down

A good relationship is built on healthy communication. When a partner is jealous, however, it is a very effective way to close those open lines of communication. Jealousy frequently necessitates one person defending themselves. When someone is defensive, they are unable to listen and reach a solution.

A downward spiral in the relationship
What you put into a relationship is usually what you get back, including jealousy. If you focus on the negative, you will only see more of it, and the Universe will reflect that back to you. Turn it around and focus on your own trust and confidence in the relationship, and you'll get more of it. "What do you want to pick?"

This is why, once identified, jealousy must be addressed immediately. Talk to your partner about your worries and find a permanent solution.

Chapter 3

Building Self-Awareness

We frequently feel as though someone is ours when we care about them. At best, we use the term "ours" as a term of endearment. At worst, we take it to an unhealthy and potentially abusive level of possessiveness. For most of us, the sense that someone belongs to us stems from our love for them, the bond we share, and the important role we play in each other's lives.

It's natural to feel envious of our partner's ex(es) from this sense of ownership. We may feel jealous in relationships because we believe the ex-partner is better than us, that our partner does not love us as much as they did another, or that they are discreetly carrying a flame for someone else.

This type of jealousy can lead to painful thought spirals and difficult emotions, undermining our confidence and the stability of our relationship. Jealousy is poisonous. It undermines the jealous person's confidence and trust in their partner, driving them away by making them feel scrutinized, defensive, and guarded.

Jealousy, as previously stated, is associated with feelings of inadequacy, low self-esteem, insecurity, and anxiety. They can be deeply ingrained and difficult to break. The practice of mindfulness, which involves bringing presence and nonjudgmental awareness to our thoughts, emotions, and experiences, can help us identify and then move past the source of our jealousy.

We can begin by mindfully re-framing our perceptions of our partner's ex(es):

Instead of viewing them as competitors, we can consider them allies. After all, they are people who love the same person we do. We don't need to communicate with them to remember them as significant figures in our partner's life. They can be viewed as past teachers who aided our partner's growth and development into the person we know and love.

Recognize the positive impact they had on our partner's life. We can appreciate what they brought into our partner's life and how it has shaped who they are today. If our partner had children with an ex, we can choose to view this as a positive result of the relationship. Perhaps the ex helped your partner through something, such as college or a major life event that was critical to your partner's current success and well-being.

Determine what your partner learned from previous relationships. I dated a man who said his ex-wife taught him how to express himself. When he told me this, I felt grateful to her for assisting him with significant emotional growth. Previous partners have taught us all valuable life and love lessons. You benefit from these experiences as your current partner for your beloved.

If changing your perspective on your partner's ex(es) does not reduce your feelings of jealousy, you may want to consider your insecurities. It's possible you have some work to do there. Healing our insecurities is an internal process, so I advise you not to look to your partner for comfort.

Take note when insecurities arise. Are they related to material aspects of your life, such as body image, money, status, the content or quality of your relationship, such as how you spend your time together, connection, relationship goals, or something else? Be inquisitive and kind. Investigate the problem as if you were a detective searching for clues.

Take steps to heal your insecurity once you've identified the source of it. This can include rewriting the story you've been telling yourself with positive self-talk, looking for and focusing on examples of how you are more than enough, and having a heart-to-heart with your companion in which you ask them to stand by you while you do this crucial healing work.

If reframing your partner's ex(es) and evaluating your insecurities aren't enough to alleviate your jealousy, you should consider outside influences. Is your partner or someone else's behavior feeding these feelings? Some of us view jealousy as a sign of love and attempt to make others jealous in order to gain power and boost our self-esteem. If any of these things are happening in your relationship, the problem is bigger than you and will require collaboration from both parties to resolve.

In and out of relationships, we all experience feelings of jealousy and insecurity. These shared experiences are a part of our humanity. Despite how common it is, jealousy is still regarded as a "bad" emotion, and many of us are ashamed of being jealous as if it indicates a personal flaw or weakness, which it does not. It's just how we're wired.

Researchers believe that jealousy serves an evolutionary purpose by strengthening the family unit and causing us to reject untrustworthy mates. Jealousy signals perceived threats and potential instability in our romantic relationships. It is our responsibility to determine whether or not these threats are real and to respond appropriately.

Jealousy, like all emotions, conveys important messages. Jealousy frequently tries to tell us that we are inadequate. This is a painful message because it threatens one of our most basic needs: acceptance.

If we examine the feeling of not being accepted, we're likely to discover that it's a lie and that we are, in fact, accepted and loved exactly as we are. If we aren't, if our partner is critical and unaccepting, we should reconsider our relationship. We not only deserve to feel loved and accepted for who we are, but it is also essential for a healthy relationship.

Working through your jealousy can help you not only heal your misconceptions about your partner's ex(es) and permanently put your insecurities to rest, but it can also help you either deepen your relationship or see where there is work to be done and make forward progress. Jealousy, like all emotions, presents a chance.

Chapter 4

Expressing Jealousy in A Healthy Way

Sometimes our feelings of jealousy are fleeting, but other times they take over and we feel compelled to express them to our partners.

The question is, how can jealousy be expressed positively? We want to express our jealousy in a healthy and constructive way, so that our feelings and concerns are heard, and the lines of interaction and confidence in the relationship are maintained.

Let's look at what feelings of jealousy in romantic relationships mean and how to talk about them with your partner.

It's perfectly normal to be envious from time to time! Jealousy can even be beneficial to a relationship, contributing to feelings of love and stability. The key is to find a positive way to express it.

To express jealousy in a constructive manner, concentrate on sharing your concerns without making accusations. Couples therapy can also aid in the exploration of feelings of jealousy that may arise in a relationship.

Feelings of jealousy are very common in relationships, whether or not your partner is doing anything to justify these feelings, such as flirting with someone else or cheating on you.

There are also lots of theories that jealousy has a biological basis, and that humans evolved to be especially protective of their romantic relationships in order to avoid infidelity.

Healthy vs. Unhealthy Jealousy

The majority of us view jealousy negatively. A jealous person is one who is anxious and insecure about their relationship. Consider a possessive, angry companion who is suspicious of every move their partner makes, whether justified or not.

While obsessive jealousy is undoubtedly unhealthy, and can sometimes lead to emotional abuse or violence, jealousy can also be a healthy emotion to experience in a relationship.

When viewed through a different lens, a jealous partner may be someone who cares deeply about their relationship and wishes to establish trust by expressing their needs and boundaries. According to studies, jealousy in relationships is associated with:

> ***Increased affection for one's partner***
> ***Increased feelings of "in love"***
> ***Increased relationship stability***

In other words, jealousy can be a healthy component of relationships when shared and expressed positively, and when shared and expressed positively, it can increase the overall happiness and longevity of the relationship.

Dealing with Infidelity in Relationships

It's important to remember that if you believe your partner is unfaithful—whether they're having sexual relations with a person behind your back, having an emotional affair, or breaking an agreed-upon rule for how to behave in your relationship—you're dealing with more than just jealousy.

If you have reason to believe that your partner has violated a serious boundary in your relationship, it is natural to feel upset and hurt; however, while you may also be experiencing jealousy, addressing this issue is not as simple as learning to express your jealousy in a healthy way.

You must also consider how to address your suspicions of infidelity in a clear and self-respecting manner. Speaking with a trusted friend or therapist ahead of time can help you do this; you might also want to think about couples therapy as a way to work through the repercussions of infidelity with your partner.

Chapter 5

Jealousy in a Healthy Context

If you are experiencing feelings of jealousy in your relationship, you do not have to repress them; in fact, doing so is not a good practice. Having said that, assaulting your partner with your feelings in a manner that is explosive or forceful is not the greatest method either.

Expressing your jealousy in a way that is honest, straightforward, and self-affirming while maintaining sensitivity to the feelings and limits of your spouse is the most healthy way to do so.

Initiate the process with some self-reflection
A number of individuals, particularly those who suffer from low self-esteem, insecurity, and anxiety, are more likely to experience feelings of jealousy than others. Irregular attachment styles and feelings of isolation are two factors that can contribute to an increased risk of experiencing envy in a romantic relationship.

You should give yourself some time to think about how you react to other relationships, behaviors, or activities that cause your spouse to feel jealous of you. It is possible that this will provide you with some insight into what is going on and what your feelings of jealousy may be trying to tell you. Think considering having a conversation about your emotions with a knowledgeable friend or a therapist.

Be resolute before the conversation begins
It's essential not to start the talk with emotions running high and inflamed, especially if you often experience envy. If possible, spend some time writing out what you want to say before the talk, since this might help you organize your thoughts.

Practice what you want to say by rehearsing alone or mimicking a discussion with a friend. Take slow breaths and meditate before the conversation, if these strategies work for you.

Share concerns, not accusations

It may be simple for your spouse to become defensive if you start listing all the things he or she does that make you envious. Focus on your feelings and concerns, not on blaming or accusing.

Consider saying "I" instead of "you."

For example: "I feel jealous when I see you ..... and I want to talk about it" is not the same as "You make me jealous when you are ......"

Say, "I want to share a particular feeling I've been having," rather than, "As of late, you've been making me very jealous."

Be patient and compassionate

Even if you talk about these thoughts in the most compassionate way imaginable, you should anticipate your spouse to have his or her own strong feelings in response. After all, you are informing him that something he is doing, or something about his relationship with you, is triggering feelings of jealousy in you.

Understandably, he may feel defensive or upset. Expect tough feelings to surface during this chat.

Just as you open up and allow your own feelings to arise, try to give your partner's feelings space. Remember that he may require time to comprehend all of this and may not instantly have a sensible (or empathetic) answer.

Give him or her time

Exposing your thoughts of envy in your relationship and your partner's reaction may take multiple conversations. The objective is that your spouse will be able to listen to your sentiments and communicate his or her own.

Your partner may be prepared to change specific behaviors that make you jealous, but the remedy may simply be the need to convince him or her that you can trust him or her to be careful of the boundaries of your relationship.

These chats can also serve to review the "rules" of the relationship so that feelings of jealousy can be kept at bay. For example, everyone flirts a little from time to time, but the amount or sort of flirtation that various partners find acceptable differs.

Some people don't mind if their partner talks about their ex-boyfriends or continues to keep a platonic relationship with them, but others do not. You and your spouse should be as explicit as possible about these types of scenarios.

Consider couples counseling
Sometimes chats with your partner regarding envy don't go as smoothly as you'd anticipated. This is understandable because jealousy is a very strong and demanding emotion. A few sessions with a therapist can help many couples get through these feelings.

Couples therapy can provide a space to vent feelings, gain more effective communication and conflict resolution skills, better understand the pressures existing in the relationship, and enhance trust.

Jealousy is a complex and uncomfortable feeling, but it regularly emerges in romantic relationships. You should not be ashamed if you experience jealousy: it is one of the emotions that makes us human. That said, it is crucial to find healthy ways to express it. As much as possible, you should start from a calm, direct, non-reactive point of view, and give your partner space to process what you're saying.

If you find it difficult to explain your sentiments to your partner or if you find it hard to talk about these concerns, you might seek individual or couples counseling.

Chapter 6

Building trust

Have you ever had the feeling that something is not right in your relationship? You may not know why, but it is most likely due to a lack of trust in your relationship. Here are the indications of a lack of trust in a relationship:

You may not trust your mate if....

> ➤ *You feel you can't let your guard down in front of your lover.*
> ➤ *You think it's best to take charge and do everything yourself.*
> ➤ *You surreptitiously watch your partner's activity on social networks.*
> ➤ *You are suspicious when he/she receives a text message.*
> ➤ *You imagine the worst when he or she doesn't answer the cell phone.*
> ➤ *Or you find it hard to ask for what you want.*

It's hard for your relationship to evolve. Worse, your relationship can seem chaotic, unpredictable, and full of drama.

The bond between trust and love is very strong. It is necessary to trust yourself, your own judgments, and others. Trust is the bedrock of any relationship. Without it, the relationship will be unstable and ultimately fail. The main reason relationships fail is a lack of trust. Because if you lack trust, you will not be confident that your partner will love and be loyal to you. After all, trust implies that you can rely on your partner, that you can confide in them, and that you feel safe with them.

Trust is important in relationships for the following reasons:

Reassurance

When you believe your partner loves you no matter what, you can be confident that your relationship will survive even if you have disagreements or fights. You know your relationship is stronger than a squabble.

Aids in the Healing of Wounds
When you are hurt in a relationship due to a misunderstanding, differing expectations, or unmet needs, trust allows you to heal and forgive.

Without trust, it is impossible to love
Trust is the cornerstone of your relationship and the key to falling in love. When you trust your partner, you can be confident that they will not abandon you in difficult times. This is the key to the development and growth of love.

Aids in Overcoming Obstacles
When you have faith in your partner, you know you are their top priority and they have your best interests at heart. When disagreements or challenges arise in your relationship, you know you can overcome them together.

Enables you to give your partner space
When you trust your partner, you are not afraid to give him time or space to do his own thing without you. You're not concerned about who he spends his time with.

Here are some indicators that you trust your partner:

Conversations are open

You're both willing to let down your guard and reveal your secrets and fears.

You are each other's number one priority.

You both prioritize each other's needs and interests. You both show concern and consideration for one another.

Make eye contact.
When you can look each other in the eyes while talking, it shows that you both have nothing to hide.

Actively listening
It demonstrates love, care, and respect if you both listen intently.

Physical closeness
It's the small things, not the big things that demonstrate how strong the bond is - a gentle kiss, holding hands, or hugging.

Making mistakes and admitting them
You are both open about your mistakes and don't try to hide them behind excuses or explanations.

Socialize with family and friends
If you enjoy socializing with each other's family and friends, it demonstrates that you both have good intentions.

Confident and at ease
When you are both your true selves around each other, it shows that you trust each other.

Resolve conflicts effectively
It demonstrates the strength of your relationship if you can both work through disagreements in healthy ways.

When you've established a trusting relationship, you'll both be free to be your true selves. However, trust must be earned. It takes some time. It does not happen automatically. It cannot be demanded. The good news is that trust can be earned through hard work. Even if your relationship has had trust issues in the past, you can change and create a trusting, secure connection.

Chapter 7

Developing Self-Esteem

Jealousy can have a negative impact on our self-esteem, making us feel inadequate. As a result, feelings of inadequacy, shame, and insecurity may arise. It can also lead to comparisons with others and a sense of being 'less than,' fueling negative self-talk and lowering self-esteem. Several strategies can be used to combat jealousy and help us focus on developing our own self-worth. *These are some examples*:

Recognizing and managing triggers

Being more aware of what causes our jealousy and taking action to reduce its intensity can assist us in shifting our focus away from the successes of others and toward our own. Redefining our triggers, learning to pause and recognize the feelings that accompany them, and engaging in activities that help us move to a more positive emotional state are all examples of this.

Practicing mindfulness

Recognizing and accepting our emotions can assist us in remaining present and forming healthy attachments with others. Focusing on our physical and mental states can help us relax and feel more in control. Developing an appreciation for the present moment and the beauty around us can also aid in the development of a sense of inner peace and self-worth.

Developing self-compassion

Engaging in nonjudgmental dialogue can aid in the development of self-trust and self-respect. Gratitude and self-care rituals such as relaxing, meditating, exercising, and getting enough sleep can boost our confidence and foster compassion and Self-Love.

Jealousy can be a destructive emotion, disrupting relationships and undermining our self-worth. However, there are strategies we can use to combat these feelings and boost our self-esteem. These include recognizing and managing our triggers, practicing mindfulness, and cultivating self-compassion. We can extend the strength and resilience required to move past feelings of jealousy and into a more positive and empowered mindset by focusing on ourselves and nurturing our self-worth.

Why Developing Self-Love Will Strengthen Your Relationship

An exceptional love does not result from two half-fulfilled people joining forces to create one whole, complete life. Outstanding love is the result of two whole people coming together to share and improve on their already full and beautiful lives.

Recently, my partner and I were talking about our relationship.

We both expressed our appreciation for the relationship. We weren't discussing how much we love each other, but rather how much we enjoy this shared space between us, which we refer to as our relationship.

We enjoy contributing to and nurturing it. We appreciate receiving it. It constantly tests us, but in the end, those tests make us better people. We believe that the relationship improves and makes us happy as individuals. We don't require it, and we don't rely on it, but we do want to keep it.

This was not always the case for me. Things started out well with previous girlfriends, but my insecurities eventually took over.

I'd lose my sense of self and become completely absorbed by the relationship. I'd come to rely on the relationship for fulfillment, happiness, validation, and self-worth. My other half was frequently struggling as well.

As a result, the positive energy in the space between us was depleted. The more desperate we both became, the more toxic it became.

We clung to each other because we thought we needed each other, but we became resentful and began to dislike the relationship. We weren't doing anything to nurture our love. We held on until things got so bad that someone snapped, and then it was over.

The distinction between then and now is self-esteem. I used to be insecure and needy, and I didn't know who I was or what I wanted out of life and love. My partners had similar issues, and my relationships inevitably deteriorated.

Now, after years of personal development and self-actualization, and with a partner who has done the same, I can truly say that I love myself and am grateful to be me.

I now love my relationship because I love myself. I don't rely on it as much as I used to, and it doesn't take away my individuality. It improves me.

It appears to be a simple concept, but it was a huge revelation for both of us during our recent conversation.

We love ourselves, we love each other, but we love this thing called "us" long after the rose-colored glasses have come off. We think the space between us is awesome as partners, teammates, friends, and lovers.

Loving Yourself While in a Relationship

It can be difficult to be in a relationship if you don't love yourself. Insecurities frequently lead to conflict, and conflict can lead to a breakup.

Before you get into a relationship, you should learn to love yourself, according to common wisdom.

But what if you're already in a relationship? Does this imply that you must separate in order to work on yourself before finding love again? Do you have to meet some arbitrary self-love requirement before you can date?

Of course, going into a relationship with a strong sense of self-love helps. But, if you're in a relationship where self-love is lacking and the space between you is needy, irritating, and harmful, I believe things can be turned around.

Learning to love oneself is an ongoing process, it's not something you can turn on and off. Even couples with a healthy amount of self-love could benefit from more.

How to Develop Self-Love in a Relationship

Maintain your freedom and independence
Allowing the relationship to absorb your identity and cause you to lose yourself as a person is unhealthy. Maintain your own rituals, activities, and social circle. Spend some quality time alone doing your own thing to nourish your soul.

Keep in mind that you are the master of your own happiness
Your partner is unable to make you happy. Only you are capable of doing so. He or she can contribute to your happiness, but it is not their responsibility to make you happy. You will drain the space between you if you rely on them for happiness.

This is not an easy task, and it is one that must be developed over time. It all starts with the mindset that happiness is a choice, which means you give yourself the ability to cultivate happiness for yourself. It's difficult and time-consuming, but it's liberating because you refuse to let your happiness be dictated by your circumstances or other people.

Choosing happiness entails accepting the axiom that the only person you have control over is yourself. Instead of attempting to change others, you focus on improving yourself and ensuring that you meet your own needs.

Another way to take charge of your happiness is to choose to be present. If you wait for the ideal circumstances before allowing yourself to be happy, you will always be waiting.

Rather than saying, "I'll be happy when...," choose happiness now. You choose to be happy in the present moment over thoughts of the past or the future.

Doing small things that make you happy can help with this. Accept the small daily opportunities to nurture yourself, such as sitting down with a cup of tea or taking ten minutes to meditate. This can help to calm your mind, allowing you to be present and find joy in your day.

Working through your past baggage can also make you feel lighter and more present, making it easier to choose happiness. However, working through past pain is an ongoing process, and while it is beneficial, it does not have to prevent you from choosing happiness.

"I'll be happy once I overcome my baggage," you don't have to say. You can be happy right now.

Consider what your partner sees in you
Insecure people struggle to see anything positive in themselves and are frequently dismissive of what their partner sees as positive.

Ask your partner what they see in you and what they like about you. This is an excellent date night activity for couples. Make a list of twenty things you admire about each other and take turns reading it aloud.

If you do this on a regular basis, you will gradually internalize it and begin to believe it about yourself.

For example, I used to judge myself harshly for being too reserved and boring. However, I've realized that my partner values my ability to maintain a level head in turbulent emotional waters.

My highs aren't that high, but neither are my lows. Instead of viewing this as a sign of weakness and something to criticize, I now see it as a sign of strength and something valuable that I bring to the relationship.

In a relationship, you are not only learning about the other person but also about yourself.

Don't be discouraged if you discover flaws in yourself
A relationship, on the other hand, will serve as a mirror to your flaws. Things about yourself that you've learned to live with may irritate your partner.

We are all flawed in some way. Some things can be ignored, while others may require your attention. In any case, don't let it bring you down or prevent you from loving yourself.

Flaws are an inevitable part of any relationship; this does not imply that you are a bad person or that you are unlovable.

Forgive yourself for your shortcomings
Holding a grudge against yourself stifles self-love. It is unavoidable in a relationship to say or do things that you later regret. Don't berate yourself for it.

Keep in mind that love is an action, not a feeling
Wise minds have always maintained that love is something you do, not something you feel. This is often said about loving another, but it also applies to loving yourself.

Even if you don't love yourself, choose to act in a self-loving manner. Make time to pamper yourself and meet your own needs.

The best way to accomplish this is to schedule "me time" on a daily basis. This is a time when you prioritize yourself over other commitments or people. Engage in simple activities that you enjoy. Going to the gym, reading the news, and eating a quiet breakfast are all things that I enjoy doing. Some people enjoy meditation, yoga, or reading.

It's all about developing a self-love ritual. One session may not make a significant difference, but if you can make it a regular daily habit, the cumulative benefits will be significant.

The early risers have convinced me that the morning is the best time to schedule this because there are no other distractions. Every day for the last year, I've gotten up an hour earlier than usual to devote to myself. You may prefer to do it in the evening as a way to unwind before bed, but make it a priority.

Keep in mind that self-love is essential for having a happy, healthy, and respectful relationship. When you are secure, confident, and happy with yourself, you radiate positive energy into the space between you. If you are having difficulties in your relationship, focus on yourself and work on self-love, and you will notice that things will improve.

Conclusion

It might not be time to end your relationship if you're experiencing jealousy. Gentle jealousy is a normal human feeling that, when handled carefully, can be advantageous. When one person feels threatened or worried about losing their partner, these emotions can change into fear, insecurity, and jealousy.

Jealousy is a perfectly normal human emotion. When handled properly, it can even be a chance to strengthen the union; however, ongoing jealousy in a relationship can indicate anxiety or self-esteem issues, such as not working through childhood issues or past infidelity, which may manifest in how you engage in your current relationship. According to research, jealousy increases when your self-esteem is threatened.

How to Handle Jealousy in a Relationship

There are many ways to manage jealousy in a relationship, whether you, your partner, or both of you are experiencing it. It's always best to be open, honest, and vulnerable with one another. Also, be open to exploring some of your own unspoken needs in order to develop a stronger sense of self-confidence. Here are some suggestions for dealing with jealousy in a relationship:

Recognize and Discuss Jealousy Openly

If you've noticed jealous feelings, it's time to have an open discussion with your partner. Communication is essential! In many cases, jealousy is an internal conflict, so engage in some introspection. Then, discuss your findings with your partner. Set boundaries for yourself and the relationship by being honest about how you feel and what makes you uncomfortable.

A partner who is open to discussing their feelings is displaying healthy jealousy. "I felt jealous when the man at the party was talking to you," for example. "I felt like he was flirting with me, and it made

34

me feel uncomfortable," is a healthy jealous expression. The way you react to your own jealousy will make or break the relationship.

Recognize that jealousy is frequently a symptom of insecurity

Jealousy is something that we have all experienced at some point in our lives. Feeling threatened by someone else is quite typical in our daily life. However, if we are not careful, jealousy can become a terrible force. Recognizing that jealousy is typically an indication of insecurity can help us be more conscious of how we feel and interact with others. If we catch ourselves growing envious, we can take a step back and reevaluate the situation. Is there anything we're terrified of? Do we feel threatened? Making the effort to identify our feelings allows us to tackle them rather than letting them fester. When we can accomplish that, we can strengthen our connections with ourselves and others.

Work on Emotional Management

Emotions can be both information and commands. That is, you can feel envy, admit how uncomfortable it is, and seek appropriate treatment without acting in a reflexive or accusatory manner. We can ask our partners for aid in relationships, but we can't expect or want them to control our emotions for us. As part of your inner work, learn to understand what you're feeling, admit it, experience it, and tolerate it.

Maintain a Relationship Journal

A journal is a secure place for you to express your feelings of jealousy, both emotionally and physically. Your notebook will not criticize you for how you feel, so use it to go beneath the surface and examine concerns and disappointments.

Reflect on your connection with the following essential questions while journaling:

- ➤ *Is your current partner genuinely the right person for you?*
- ➤ *Did they do anything in particular to trigger the jealousy?*
- ➤ *Is your history interfering with your new relationship?*
- ➤ *Are you sabotaging yourself?*

Look within before pointing fingers

We all have various life experiences that impact our relationship expectations. Past experiences in family, friends, and romantic relationships might contribute to feelings of distrust, insecurity, or dependency in the present. Making charges against your partner can make them defensive or even insecure. When feelings of jealousy arise, it's wise to take a minute to pause and reflect on what in your background is provoking you to presume the worst about your spouse. You can then use I-statements to clarify how and why you are feeling, without leaping to conclusions or assigning blame. This vulnerability might actually bring you and your partner closer together as you discover more about each other's needs.

Investigate the Root Causes

Determine the root of your feelings before communicating with your partner. Accept responsibility for your behaviors and make a commitment to coping with your fears.

One technique for dealing with low self-esteem is to define personal values such as communication, compassion, or honesty. This allows you to recognize your positive features and reflect on what is important to you in the relationship. This could assist in lessening the relationship's painful feelings of envy and overthinking.

It may not necessarily suggest that your partner is acting inappropriately

If envy presents itself in your life, you may perceive it as a warning sign that something is amiss. Have you ever heard someone say, "I suspected he was cheating on me, that's the reason I checked his cell?" Many people rapidly believe their intuition when it tells them that their union boundaries are being crossed when they see overlaps between other people's actions and sentiments. However, jealousy alone does not properly identify cheating or other disrespectful actions. It could signal that you are terrified of anything happening, even if it is not already happening. You can utilize this as information without instantly acting on it!"

Determine Unmet Needs

This can be difficult since you will have to practice being vulnerable. When envy involves a third party, you should undertake a self-evaluation to help you navigate through the emotional maze. You don't want to make assumptions or bring up prior difficulties or experiences and put them into your current relationship.

Self-evaluation can be as simple as asking yourself the following questions:

> ➤ *What is the emotion attempting to tell me?*
> ➤ *In this relationship, where do I feel invisible?*
> ➤ *What am I no longer getting out of this connection that I believe this other person is?*
> ➤ *What do I believe I'm losing?*

Taking the time to contemplate and answer these questions can reveal unfulfilled needs. After you've got this fresh viewpoint, you may determine how you wish to respond to your sentiments.

Express Your Concerns

If your partner's acts or the conduct of others towards your relationship provoke jealousy, don't be hesitant to bring it up with your partner as soon as possible. They could have been unconscious of the action, or they could have been unaware of how you felt. Take advantage of this time to discuss or reconsider any relationship boundaries.

If you trust your spouse but have reservations due to previous relationship experiences, try to discover ways for both of you to remedy the issue. Keep in mind that your spouse has chosen to be with you. For example, if you are jealous of someone in your partner's life, consider muting their Instagram account so you have fewer opportunities to compare yourself to them.

Avoid Making Hasty Decisions

In the middle of temporarily heightened emotions, the decisions you make can have long-term negative implications. Jealousy that swings out of control might emerge as anger, causing the relationship to fall apart. When you are emotionally aroused by envy, it is strongly advised that you take a few minutes to self-soothe.

Begin to Value Yourself More
Low self-esteem and insecurity are two of the most prominent reasons for envy. There's this dreadful notion that you're not good enough for your lover. Some people are envious because they believe they live in the shadow of their partner's ex. These reasons will naturally make you feel as if the relationship and your self-esteem are under threat.

A smart way is to compile a list of everything you appreciate about yourself and everything your spouse likes about you. Allow your spouse to assist you with this list. Another thing you can do, especially if you find yourself continually comparing yourself to others, is to go through your social media accounts, such as Instagram, and unfollow persons who make you feel uneasy. This can help you acquire distance from emotions of inferiority and, in time, increase your self-esteem.

Develop Healthy Coping Skills
Coping with sparked jealousy will not help you work through the underlying difficulties, but moving your attention away from it will help you avoid acting on your sentiments in a damaging way.

Among the effective coping exercises are:

- *Exercising your deep breathing*
- *Muscle relaxation that is gradual*
- *A meditation exercise*

Heal the Wounds of Your Past
Another reason you may be envious is a lack of trust from previous relationships. Trust issues are typically the outcome of poor or painful past events, such as infidelity in previous love relationships. Lack of confidence in your partner, on the other side, may lead to the

prospect of controlling them. Having some control is normal, but trying to control your spouse for matters over which you have no control is troublesome and destructive to the relationship.

The first step in overcoming these trust issues and overall personal growth is to learn to heal your scars. This can help you trust your partner more and stop attempting to control every element of the relationship. Remember that the person you're with is not your ex-partner whenever you feel envious. Let go of control and trust.

Consult a Therapist

If you're having problems dealing with envious thoughts/feelings on your own, don't be hesitant to get help from a therapist. Talking about envy isn't always easy, and you could feel even more uneasy at first, but an excellent therapist understands that jealousy is normal and will respond to you with empathy and compassion.

Here are several symptoms that you should consult a therapist:

- *Obsessive or obsessed thoughts are triggered by jealousy.*
- *Jealousy becomes obtrusive or overpowering.*
- *Violent feelings or impulses*
- *Problematic activities, such as continuously following, spying on, or monitoring your spouse on social media*

Jealousy has a bad impact on your daily life and hinders you from focusing on your job, activities, and so on.

Consider Couples Therapy

Jealousy manifests itself in numerous ways, but it is primarily caused by a lack of communication. Couples therapy might help you see that your envy is either illogical or the product of a misunderstanding. A couples therapist can help you to be sensitive and understand why your partner is acting the way they are rather than automatically concluding that they are attracted to someone else.

A couples therapist may also utilize cognitive behavioral therapy (CBT) to educate you and your partner on how to detect negative, intrusive thoughts, challenge their validity, and replace them with more realistic, supportive thoughts. "He is going to leave me for his coworker," for example, would be replaced with "He is friendly and professional with all of his coworkers because they work together." When feelings of envy are not ridiculed or shamed, working together can bring spouses closer together.

How to Handle a Jealous Partner

Being in a relationship with a jealous partner isn't always a deal breaker. Some people have trust issues that arise from previous relationships or breakups, and open communication, good boundaries, and patience can help couples work through these challenges. *Advices for handling a partner who is jealous:*

Discuss their issues and worries

Take a seat and ask them directly what's going on. Because jealousy shows that a person feels threatened or terrified, it's vital that you listen with respect and compassion without discounting their feelings, especially if you know your partner suffers from anxiety.

Don't be defensive about your own activities

This will most certainly be difficult but try to appraise the situation and respond to your partner gently. Assure them that you want to work with them to fix the problem. If you're thinking of terminating the relationship, now might be a good moment to talk about it.

Exhibit extra affection

Give your partner more physical affection during this sensitive period to show your love. Even if their envy appears illogical to you, it is vital that you stay supportive.

Establish healthy boundaries

Setting firm limits is a worthwhile investment in your relationship. It's acceptable to tolerate mild jealousy from a spouse, but if it escalates or becomes abusive, you should get help straight away. If you are being mistreated, it is vital to explain the behaviors you are prepared to work through as well as those you have zero tolerance for.

Be patient and return to the problem
Jealousy is a problem that will require time and effort to resolve. It
will be time-consuming and emotionally draining at times, but it is
vital that you remain supportive, seek to create trust, and make it
apparent that you are dedicated to working together to address the
problem.

Jealousy is a normal human emotion that needs to be expressed.
Jealousy in a relationship may simply suggest that you need to talk
with your partner about your needs, insecurities, boundaries, and
desires. Healthy jealousy that is honestly communicated contributes
to relationship growth. This could look like one partner detecting
fears and adopting a method to deal with them.

Healthy jealousy and unhealthy jealousy are the two sorts of
jealousy. Healthy jealousy emerges from identifying a potential threat
and the need to defend a partner you care about. This is entirely
normal and a natural element of being human. If, on the other hand,
jealousy is caused by fear and leads to actions based on mistrust,
paranoia, or insecurity, it is unhealthy and not based on love.

Jealousy in relationships has been connected to qualities such as
low self-esteem, insecurity, feelings of inadequacy, and emotional
reliance. It can be a complicated emotion produced by a lot of
circumstances such as abandonment issues, being cheated on in the
past, or not feeling good enough/worthy. The best coping method is
to research and heal the underlying problem.

Most partnerships encounter envy at some point, and if it is
addressed openly, it can eventually benefit your connection. How
you deal with your own envy can make or break a relationship. Take
charge of your emotions by sharing them with your spouse and
actively pursuing solutions to work through them.

If you're ready to start looking for a therapist, consider using an
internet directory to find the best fit for you. Check with friends,
family, and coworkers. Many people are in therapy and can provide

recommendations. Others may be aware of reputable therapists in your region or resources that can connect you with therapists.

Working with a skilled therapist can help you negotiate and overcome the obstacles of being in a relationship with a jealous partner in a helpful and nonjudgmental manner. Remember that you are not alone.